DISCOVERING AND DEVELOPING A PASSION FOR GOD

DAVID LEE MARTIN

—

FREE TABERNACLE PRAYER
GUIDE & VIDEO WORKSHOP

Please accept this free gift
www.davidleemartin.net/tabernacle-prayer-guide

Your free illustrated guide to Tabernacle Prayer, leading you step-by-step through this powerful pathway to the Father's presence.

Also includes Free Access to a in-depth online prayer workshop.

Recorded at a full day of Tabernacle Prayer teaching and activation, these powerful video sessions lead the listener through the gates of the Heavenly Tabernacle on a revelation filled journey into the Holy of Holies.

You will learn to pray Tabernacle Prayer with 4 hours of in depth revelatory teaching, activation and life-changing testimony.

Join David For A Life-Changing Revelation of Prayer and Encounter With God
www.davidleemartin.net/tabernacle-prayer-guide

THE HUNGRY SOUL

"And there is no one who calls on Your name, who stirs himself up to take hold of You; for You have hidden Your face from us, and have consumed us because of our iniquities."

— ISAIAH 64:7, NKJV.

"With my soul I have desired You in the night, yes, by my spirit within me I will seek You early; for when your judgments are in the earth, the inhabitants of the world will learn righteousness."

— ISAIAH 26:9, NKJV.

INTRODUCTION

WORDS FROM A FELLOW TRAVELER...

From the outset I made the decision to share my journey in God with others. What this means is that thankfully I do not have to reach some fevered state of perfection before putting my thoughts and experiences on paper. Every day is a day in which we can grow, and the expectation is that things will change, and grow as I go along.

Developing a Passion for God is one of the very first books I wrote. Now, almost ten years later, I find many of the principles are still ones I put to use every day of my life. I have also added new insights that I believe will be helpful for my fellow travelers. I hope that the same fire that infused the words of the original continue to burn brightly, and ignite a determination in your heart to go for more of God.

This book is still a quick and easy read, but as dangerous to the devil as a piece of spiritual dynamite. Be careful - the words on these pages are intended to ignite a fresh hunger in your heart that you won't be able to shake until you take it to the prayer closet!

We live in a time where people are certainly in passionate pursuit, but the chase seems to be more for fame and fortune than for holiness and revival. We live in a culture caught up in a cultic worship of celebrity, and the ancient fires that blazed in the hearts of past revivalists is sorely absent.

As Leonard Ravenhill said, "The early church was married to poverty, prisons and persecutions. Today, the church is married to prosperity, personality, and popularity."

Singing a few choruses on Sunday morning, and rehearsing a handful of polite, passionless prayers, will never cut through the bulwarks of unbelief that presently hinder the move of God's Spirit. It requires something far more incendiary.

I will share with honest simplicity some of the keys that I have used to stir my own heart toward God. As Isaiah urges, we must stir ourselves to seek Him, to expect His power and presence in heavenly response. Spirituality is intended to be simple. Papa has not placed barriers between Himself and His children. The principles of the Spirit are not difficult to grasp. The mind of the flesh looks for complexity, hoops to jump through to earn God's respect and response. The man of the Spirit on the other hand has embraced the fact that God requires little from us other than sincere childlike faith exercised through simple obedience to His Word.

If we will draw near to Him, He will surely draw near to us!

This is not intended to be a book that offers nice tidy solutions. It will raise more questions that it offers answers. But it will drive you, the reader, to take those unspoken longings to the only place they can find some relief - the presence of God in private fervent prayer.

Jesus is the only hope for a dying world, but if the embers in the hearts of His lovers are snuffed by the desire for other things, who will bring that burning message to the world?

We need revival, and it must begin in the chambers of our own hearts!

PART I
HUNGER

"The hallmark of every revival is hunger of heart; the heart's pursuit of a personal relationship with Christ, the hearts longing to experience God's presence, and the heart's cry to worship God in spirit and in truth. Revival is the product of an awakening of the heart to the power and presence of the living Christ who loves us unconditionally."

— ROBERTS LIARDON, GOD'S GENERALS, THE REVIVALISTS

ACKNOWLEDGE YOUR HUNGER

"THE SOUL MUST LONG FOR GOD IN ORDER
TO BE SET AFLAME BY GOD'S LOVE; BUT IF
THE SOUL CANNOT YET FEEL THE
LONGING, THEN IT MUST LONG FOR THE
LONGING. TO LONG FOR THE LONGING IS
ALSO FROM GOD." — MEISTER ECKHART

> "Blessed are those who hunger and thirst
> for righteousness, For they shall be filled."
>
> — MATTHEW 5:6, NKJV

We must acknowledge our hunger for the things of God. Recognizing that there is an emptiness inside your life apart from Him is how you took your first step to salvation, and your progress in the things of the Spirit will happen in precisely the same way. Through hunger.

One of my all time favorite verses (I have many) is found in Ecclesiastes chapter three. Verse 11 reads:

> "He has made everything beautiful in it's time. He also has planted eternity in men's hearts and minds [a divinely implanted sense of a purpose working through the ages which nothing under the sun but God alone can satisfy]..."
>
> — ECCLESIASTES 3:11 AMPLIFIED

As Jesus explained in the verse you read from Matthew at the outset of this chapter, first comes the hunger, then comes the filling. The longing you feel in your soul for God is planted by Him. It is an eternal seed that only an eternal Being can satisfy. People run themselves ragged trying to plug the hole with temporal solutions, but it is God alone who can truly answer the deepest cry of the human heart.

SMORGASBORD SPIRITUALITY

I remember as a teenager having a very real hunger for spiritual experiences. I had a clear sense of something greater at work in the universe than that which can be apprehended by the natural senses. That invisible seed was in my heart but I had no idea where it had come from. Certainly, at that time,

Jesus Christ did not seem much of an option in comparison to the smorgasbord of religions and spiritual paths that were on offer. In my ignorance I could not understand why anyone would limit themselves to one way, when you could grab as many as you wanted and cobble together a spirituality of your own making.

My problem was that I was not looking at Jesus.

At that time my idea and experience of Christianity, the religion that bears Christ's name, was that it was a dead and lifeless institution. The outward pomp and ceremony of the 'church' completely veiled the living reality of Jesus from even the keenest spiritual seeker. It seemed that there was more power and spirituality on display in the local new age wholesaler than in any of the churches that I had come across at that time. Nevertheless, I did begin reading the New Testament. I was reading many 'spiritual' books so it seemed only fair to give the Christian book a fair go.

Amazingly, as I feasted upon what was really said about Jesus, my whole outlook changed. He is the jigsaw piece that completes the picture. He is the cog that fits to make the machinery of life work. Jesus

was the answer to the spiritual satisfaction my heart
craved.

I was on a genuine search for truth, and I found
Him. More accurately, He found me.

> "Ye have not chosen me, but I have
> chosen you…"

— JOHN. 15:16 KJV

Jesus is the Way, the Truth (the Reality) and the Life.

He is God!

My search both ended and began at the very
moment I accepted Jesus for who He is - the Son of
the Living God, Savior of the world.

On a more personal level - my Savior. And yours.

CHRISTIANITY IS PERSONAL

Christianity has to become personal for it to really
work in your life. Why? Because God is a Person.
Jesus did not die to a start a new religion. He saw a
joy before Him and willingly went to the cross
because He wanted a personal relationship with you.

Before my encounter with Jesus Christ, my hunger for reality drove me to seek in all the wrong places. I was looking for experiences, doctrines, teachings and enlightenments. What does this book or that great teacher say? What experiences can I have that will bring me closer to spiritual enlightenment?

But it is not a *What* we are looking for, it is a *Who*!

Coming to Christ was only the beginning of the great adventure that I have now enjoyed for over 25 years. I now know Who I am seeking, and I never come to the end of His wonders. Constantly I am awed at the breadth and length and depth and height of His love. His wisdom is indeed unsearchable. The deeper you go the greater the depths you realize there are to plumb.

Jesus is the object of my passion. I seek to know more of Him. Where all other wells run dry, He, and He alone, is the "well of water, springing up into everlasting life."

Acknowledging your spiritual hunger leads first to the cross, and onward toward the desire to see God's mighty resurrection power displayed in your life through relationship with Jesus.

Stirring passion begins as simply as this; accepting that our heart is unsatisfied with the status quo. Confessing to ourselves that we haven't arrived, that we need more, and a refusal to settle for anything less than God's best.

God has not chosen you for an emaciated experience of His love and power. He has called you to know and experience Him in powerful, transformative encounters.

Consider this prayer of Paul, fully expressing God's infinite desire for you. Please don't pass it over, read it in full, slowly and prayerfully. I have highlighted part of Paul's prayer, but every single letter of these verses is aflame with the passionate love of Father, Son and Holy Ghost:

> "May He grant you out of the rich treasury of His glory to be strengthened and reinforced with mighty power in the inner man by the [Holy] Spirit [Himself indwelling your innermost being and personality]. May Christ through your faith [actually] dwell (settle down, abide, make His permanent home) in your hearts! May you be rooted deep in love

and founded securely on love, That you may have the power and be strong to apprehend and grasp with all the saints [God's devoted people, the experience of that love] what is the breadth and length and height and depth [of it]; **[That you may really come] to know [practically, through experience for yourselves] the love of Christ, which far surpasses mere knowledge [without experience]; that you may be filled [through all your being] unto all the fullness of God [may have the richest measure of the divine Presence**, and become a body wholly filled and flooded with God Himself]!"

— EPHESIANS 3:16-19

Does your experience live up to this lofty possibility? Is there not more still waiting for you to discover?

Knowing just how incredible the reality is that we have been invited into should so stir our hearts. It should provoke you to rebel against the flavorless religion that has been foisted upon so many unsuspecting saints, and cause you to pray and seek

Him like Jacob, refusing to let go until you genuinely experience the depths of His love.

Friend and fellow firebrand, there is more!

Notes & References Relevant to what you have just been reading. Take some time to look up each verse in your own Bible.

Matthew 5:6; Ecclesiastes 3:11 Amplified Bible; John 14:6; Ephesians 3:18-19; Romans 11:33; John 4:14; Jeremiah 2:13; Philippians 3:8-11

SPEAK YOUR HUNGER

"WORDS ARE CONTAINERS FOR POWER,
YOU CHOOSE WHAT KIND OF POWER THEY
CARRY." — JOYCE MEYER

God's ways are very simple. He has not concocted complex hoops that we are forced to jump through to connect and engage with His power.

Sometimes the avenues He offers are so ordinary that we miss them. The natural man is always looking for something to boast in. God's ways on the other hand are so incredibly simple that even a child can engage in them.

Why do I say this? Because pride wants some high-sounding revelation to brag about.

I have no such thing to offer you.

My advice to those of you who sincerely want to develop a life-transforming hunger for heaven is simply this...

To develop your hunger for God you must speak it out.

Your lips are like the rudder that steers the ship of your life. James points out that although the rudder is small it turns a great vessel whatever way it will *(James 3:4)*. Our tongue is like that rudder, and our appetites follow the words that we indulge ourselves in. Just as we choose what goes into our mouth, perhaps more importantly we also choose what comes out.

Often our appetites are so tuned to the world. So many years of living in a society that exalts possession over sacrifice, selfishness over love, and comfort over courage has oftentimes dulled our senses to the spirit world.

In your prayer closet, walk the floor declaring your hunger for God. Speak out your desire to see His Kingdom come. Build upon your hunger through the confession of your mouth.

Romans 10 holds keys that reveal how to release our faith.

> "that if you confess with your mouth the Lord Jesus and believe in your heart that God has raised Him from the dead, you will be saved. For with the heart one believes unto righteousness, and with the mouth confession is made unto salvation."

— ROMANS 10:9,10, NKJV

Again in 2 Corinthians 4:13:

> "And since we have the same spirit of faith, according to what is written, "I believed and therefore I spoke," we also believe and therefore speak,"

— 2 CORINTHIANS 4:13, NKJV

What we believe in our heart, all that is alive in our spirit, must be spoken out. Vocalizing what God has planted in you gives substance to the seed. Prayer waters the seed planted so God's Holy Spirit can go to work to bring supernatural increase.

DEATH & LIFE

Your words are powerful. They are carriers in the spirit world reaching out and demanding what they ask for. Proverbs 18:21 goes so far as to say that death and life reside in the tongue. This unforgettable verse teaches that we will eat the fruit of the words we indulge in, for good or for bad.

> "Death and life are in the power of the tongue, and they who indulge in it shall eat the fruit of it [for death or life]"
>
> — PROVERBS 18:21 AMPLIFIED

It is through confession that life is breathed onto our desires. On our breath the power and purpose of God's Word is released into our lives. Just as the Holy Spirit was found brooding over the formless waters in Genesis awaiting life-giving word to be spoken, so it it with the brooding desires of your heart. The Holy Spirit is waiting for you to bring life to those God-planted desires through words of faith.

Maybe you are not hungry for God, or maybe, like me, you are aware that your hunger could be so much greater and far-reaching. Walk the floor confessing your hunger until it comes like a flood, knowing that you will eat the fruit of your lips. As you do this you will build a spiritually receptive atmosphere around your heart prepared and ready for God to speak.

Often the desires of our born-again spirit are opposed by the flesh. In fact, I think the flesh is more of an enemy to personal revival than the devil himself. Satan is dethroned and ultimately powerless, but so much of our old nature continues to hold sway in our lives.

Paul says of this in Galatians 5:17:

> "For the flesh lusts against the Spirit, and the Spirit against the flesh; and these are contrary to one another, so that you do not do the things that you wish."
>
> — GALATIANS 5:17, NKJV

We must give voice to the longings of our spirit in order to quench the desires of our flesh. If necessary use your lips not only to invite the things of God, but also to relinquish the grip of worldliness on your affections.

Let your mouth lead the way to a new place in God's purposes for your life and family.

Speak it out...

"Lord, I'm hungry. I'm hungry for You. I want more of You. More of Your power. I want to see You move in our land, in my life. God, I'm hungry for Your presence. To know You is my highest desire. I forsake all and follow You. I reject the grip that the world has on my affections. I will not seek fulfillment apart from your will. You are my satisfaction. I'm hungry for Your Spirit in my life. Hungry to see Your power in my family, my church, my city and my nation..."

As you begin praying prayers like this your heart will follow, reaching out in faith for fulfillment. Hunger will be stirred and new appetites for heaven's realities will be cultivated.

Notes & References Relevant to what you have just been reading:

Romans 10:9-10; 2 Corinthians 4:13; Mark 11:22-25; Galatians 5:17

FEED YOUR HUNGER

"IF YOU DON'T FEEL STRONG DESIRES FOR
THE MANIFESTATION OF THE GLORY OF
GOD, IT IS NOT BECAUSE YOU HAVE DRUNK
DEEPLY AND ARE SATISFIED. IT IS
BECAUSE YOU HAVE NIBBLED SO LONG AT
THE TABLE OF THE WORLD. YOUR SOUL IS
STUFFED WITH SMALL THINGS, AND
THERE IS NO ROOM FOR THE GREAT." —
JOHN PIPER, A HUNGER FOR GOD

"Your words were found, and I ate them,
And Your word was to me the joy and
rejoicing of my heart; For I am called by
Your name, O LORD God of hosts."

— JEREMIAH 15:16, NKJV

What we feed will grow. What we starve will die. What are you feeding? Your spirit life or your flesh life?

How do we feed our inner man? The answer of surprisingly simple; Through your eyes and your ears.

What are you allowing into your spirit and soul through your eyes and ears?

Matthew 5:6, says:

> "Blessed are those who hunger and thirst for righteousness, For they shall be filled."

Righteousness is God's way of doing, thinking and being. I once heard a preacher say something that really struck me. He was talking about spiritual hunger and said, *"If there is a hunger, it is because there is something to satisfy that hunger."* In other words, the existence of a hunger indicates the existence of the thing sparking that hunger.

Hungry for change and transformation in your life? The very existence of that desire speaks to the real possibility of it coming to pass.

Looking for citywide awakening? Would God plant a seed with no intention of fulfillment?

The desire does not guarantee satisfaction, and as we are all aware there are multitudes of desires, even very good and noble ones, that go unanswered. But Papa doesn't plant desires to frustrate us.

The seed is sown to prompt the heart to pray.

This is where many fall. They feel the passion, sense the hunger, are stirred by the vision, but never take it to the birthing room of fervent prayer.

If you are hungry for an awesome revival that sweeps your nation it's because it is a real possibility in the spirit realm. If you thirst for radical life-changing encounters with God's presence, or for your family and community to be gloriously saved, it is because it can happen, if you seek it with all your heart. The hunger is there to provoke prayer until it comes to pass.

Hunger is merely the prompt. Prayer is the response.

STIR YOUR SPIRITUAL APPETITE

This is the stumbling block many of us face. We have a hunger, but it never translates into passionate action in the prayer closet. We need to develop our hunger first to the point where we cannot stand not to pray, and then to the place where it propels us to persevere until we see and experience the results of those prayers and petitions.

So how do we develop a hunger in the first place?

If you've ever fasted I'm sure that you will recognize the dynamic of desire that goes to work. You're doing great until you walk past your favorite delicatessen. The invisible aromas carried on the breeze leave your taste buds dancing and your flesh screaming.

Just as in the natural world aromas provoke us to desire, so in the spirit.

There are aromas in the spirit realm of revival, salvation, deliverance, freedom. As we dampen the cravings of our natural man the senses of our spirit heighten and we catch the wind of God's Spirit. On that wind He carries the purposes of God for individuals and nations. As we sniff the goodness of God on the breeze, we catch them in the spirit, and are awakened to faith and propelled to pray.

SO MUCH BETTER THAN A DONUT

Your appetite for spiritual things is awakened and heightened when natural cravings are dampened and brought into subjection. Your spirit man beings to salivate, seeking to be satisfied with Heaven's harvest.

But you must turn your affections and appetites away from the things of this world. Spiritual appetites are not accidental. They are developed through intentional focus.

God told Joshua:

> "Only be strong and very courageous, that you may observe to do according to all the law which Moses My servant commanded you; **do not turn from it to the right hand or to the left, that you may prosper wherever you go. This Book of the Law shall not depart from your mouth, but you shall meditate in it day and night**, that you may observe to do according to all that is written in it. For then you will make your way prosperous, and then you will have good success."
>
> — JOSHUA 1:7,8, NKJV

Keep your eyes on Jesus. Many schemes are devised to get our eyes off God. If you are a Television addict, switch the TV off! If sport consumes your thought life trim it down. Ration yourself, don't buy sport magazines, don't discuss the latest game with everyone you meet. Whatever your weakness, you can choose to either feed it or to starve it. What you feed will grow, what you starve will eventually weaken its hold on your affections.

Conversely, feed your spirit. A taste for spiritual things is fortified by ingesting truth. My daughter was an elite gymnast for several years, and is now a professional ballet dancer. As such she has a strict diet comprising only foods that provide the energy and nutrition that the demands of her active life require of her.

The foods that she eats today were not the ones she would have chosen ten years ago. In fact, when she first started restricting what she ate it felt unpleasant. The 'empty' calories that she once craved have been replaced today with a desire for only foods that feed her need for strength.

How did this change occur? By disciplining herself to eat what at first she did not want to. Her flesh wanted ice cream, but her body needed fruit.

As she applied herself diligently her tastes have changed.

YOUR APPETITE GROWS AS YOUR GIVE YOURSELF TO THE THINGS OF GOD

I promise you, if you discipline yourself to read and study the Scriptures, and to spend time in prayer, your taste and craving for these spiritual disciplines will transform them into a delight.

Spiritual hunger is far less mysterious that most people think. They excuse their lukewarm approach to the things of God, thinking that the initiative should come from Him. If God wants to touch me He can, they reason. All the while Father is waiting for us to approach Him.

He may have sought us out when we were groping in spiritual darkness, but now that we are in the light it is our prerogative to turn our hearts toward the things of eternity and fervently pursue them.

This often requires strong decisions to be made regarding where we turn our hearts, and the activities and thoughts we give ourselves over to.

> "But if thine heart turn away, so that thou wilt not hear, but shalt be drawn away, and worship other gods, and serve them; I denounce unto you this day, that ye

shall surely perish, *and that* ye shall not prolong *your* days upon the land, whither thou passest over Jordan to go to possess it. I call heaven and earth to record this day against you, *that* I have set before you life and death, blessing and cursing: therefore choose life, that both thou and thy seed may live: That thou mayest love the LORD thy God, *and* that thou mayest obey his voice, and that thou mayest cleave unto him: for he *is* thy life, and the length of thy days: that thou mayest dwell in the land which the LORD sware unto thy fathers, to Abraham, to Isaac, and to Jacob, to give them."

— DEUTERONOMY 30:17–20 KJV

Notes & References Relevant to what you have just been reading:

Jeremiah 15:16; Matthew 5:6; 2 Corinthians 2:14-15; Joshua 1:7-8; Deuteronomy 30:17-20

FEED ON HEAVEN'S MANNA

"WE MUST NOT SELECT A FEW FAVORITE
PASSAGES TO THE EXCLUSION OF OTHERS.
NOTHING LESS THAN A WHOLE BIBLE CAN
MAKE A WHOLE CHRISTIAN." — A.W.
TOZER

Feed the spiritual side of your life. Read good books that expand your vision of what is possible. Watch videos and TV that will edify, encourage and fuel the fire of God burning in your heart. Ungodly literature and conversation are like water on the fire. Wholesome and Godly counsel is like gasoline!

Paul says in Galatians 6:8;

> "For he who sows to his flesh will of the flesh reap corruption, but he who sows to the Spirit will of the Spirit reap everlasting life."

— GALATIANS 6:8, NKJV

I have noticed that if I neglect Bible reading and prayer (sowing to the Spirit) and watch too much TV or too many movies (sowing to the flesh) it corrupts my life with God. It corrupts my hunger for the things of God and the move of God. However, during seasons of prayer, fasting and study, not only is my hunger satisfied, it is intensified. The more I get the more I want. The more I seek, the more I find, the more I am provoked to seek even further.

God's rich and wonderful undeserved graces are unfathomable.

READING IS FEEDING

One of the most effective ways to develop a hungry passion for God is to read. I was never much of a reader in my youth, but from about age 16, I began to develop a real love for the written word. It is here that I feed the fire in my spirit with life-giving fuel.

Jesus said in John 6:63:

> "It is the Spirit who gives life; the flesh profits nothing. The words that I speak to you are spirit, and they are life."

Words are powerful. They are like containers that when opened spill their contents into the soul and imagination, and into your spirit.

If you read books about great men and women of faith, and moves of God, it develops a thirst in your soul to see the same. Often our imaginations are restricted by the limited experience of God in our own lives and congregations. Undoubtedly, many of these things will be good and significant, however, it is essential that we stretch the tent pegs of our mind and embrace the possibility of more. One way to do this is by feeding your spirit with stories of past moves of God, and allowing your heart to project those visions onto your own community and nation.

Get hold of some books about the Lewis revival in Scotland under Duncan Campbell. Read some of Charles Finney's own accounts of the revivals that he was involved in. Study the awesome ministry of the Booth's and the Salvation Army in their heyday. One of the most moving for me are the accounts of the Fulton Street Prayer Revival in 1857.

Friend, these accounts cannot fail but stir a hunger to see again the things that others have experienced. Fill your library with books by tried and tested God chasers; A W Tozer, T L Osborn, Kathryn Kuhlman,

Andrew Murray, E M Bounds, Oswald J Smith, Watchman Nee, to name just a few. Allow the experiences of others to propel you onward toward God's zealous purpose for your life and ministry.

Don't settle for what you know to be less than God's best. Build pictures of possibility on the inside and pray them into manifestation.

If books are not your thing, listen to audio or watch video. Check out sermonindex.net for hundreds of free audio sermons by revivalists present and past. One way or another, it is essential that you feed your spiritual life with edifying material and fire baptized words.

Ensure that you give precedence to the scriptures themselves. Take time to read and meditate in the Word of God. Look into the life of Jesus. Glean from the accounts of others who have gone before. Learn methods of study and become a student of God's Word, building it systematically into your life. Ask God each time you read to help you understand it, and allow the Holy Spirit to enlighten your mind. Most importantly of all, act upon what He shows you.

BIBLICAL ILLITERACY

I am always amazed, and somewhat dismayed, at how few Christians ever undertake a thorough study of the Scriptures in a systematic way. The Biblical illiteracy that is present in many of our churches is shocking.

God has provided all we need, but how many fail to avail themselves of the promises simply because they do not even know what they are!

Of all the recommendations I can offer you with regard to developing a root of righteousness and an unquenchable longing for God it would be this - fall in love with the Scriptures.

The words of the Bible are supernatural. They change a man or a woman from the inside out.

There are numerous avenues to accomplish this, and they do not necessarily require that you attend a college or make radical decisions that affect what you are already doing in your life. One way would be to sign up for the school that I developed. It is a complete and thorough study of all the major doctrines and books of the Bible, in an easy to access online school that you consume at your own pace and to fit with your necessary schedule. Here's the link, and it's totally free, https://www.davidleemartin.net/the-spirit-life-bible-school

Listen to heart-stirring teaching and preaching as you travel or cook or workout at the gym. Look for places already existing in your schedule that provide windows of possibility to feed your spirit. It make take choices and creativity, but no one is in a position where they cannot invite more of God's word into their every day life.

Make the decision to invest in your spiritual growth in the same way that you invest to develop your professional, educational and social life. All of us pour finance, time, thought and energy into these aspects of our life. How much more important is your spiritual growth than the natural? Yet our time and money flies in every other direction.

I say, enough with my excuses! Enough with my pandering!

I love Paul's admonition to Timothy:

> "For physical training is of some value (useful for a little), but godliness (spiritual training) is useful *and* of value in

everything *and* in every way, for it holds promise for the present life and also for the life which is to come."

— 1 TIMOTHY 4:8 AMPLIFIED

Investment in your spiritual growth and maturity reaps eternal results, but the seeds of those results are sown little-by-little on a daily basis. I apply the same principle in my physical exercise regime, and have found that little and often yields excellent and marked results.

DON'T WAIT FOR A CHANGE, MAKE A CHANGE

Too many well-meaning believers are waiting for a cataclysmic change to hit their busy schedule before they spend time with God. It is easy to deceive yourself into thinking that if you don't spend several hours then it is not worth spending any time. If 5 minutes is all you have, give those 5 to seek Him. If your hour-long drive to work is usually spent on frivolous radio shows turn your dashboard into an altar and use the time for prayer.

Look for opportunities that already exist and harness them.

Be intentional. Set aside specific time to seek and pray. Build a life of prayer, rather than just appending a few hurried prayers to your over-active calendar.

(If I may, I would like to recommend a companion volume in this series, *Discovering and Developing a Secret Life of Prayer*. This short book digs deep into the process of developing your personal prayer life.)

Don't waste another day waiting for some titanic revelation to rock your world - take a simple, manageable step this day, and every day that follows, and you will see tangible growth and breakthrough faster than you might expect.

The Spirit Life Bible School could provide the spiritual nutrition required for the next stages in your journey for many months and even years to come. I'm honestly not trying to sell you on something, just genuinely urging you to take your spiritual life seriously, and offering just one of the many excellent avenues you might follow to make that happen.

The school is available at https://www.davidleemartin.net/the-spirit-life-bible-school and will be one of the best investments of time you ever make!

Notes & References Relevant to what you have just been reading:

Galatians 6:8; John 6:63; Isaiah 54:2; 2 Timothy 2:15; Ephesians 1:17-20; Romans 15:4; Proverbs 2:1-6; John 16:13; 1 John 2:27; James 1:25

MIGHTY MOVES

Mighty moves of God require mighty movements of the soul in prayer. Deep cries that dredge the heart of every other desire and affection.

We pray...

> "Oh that thou wouldest rend the heavens, that thou wouldest come down, that the mountains might flow down at thy presence, As *when* the melting fire burneth, the fire causeth the waters to boil, to make thy name known to thine adversaries, *that* the nations may tremble at thy presence!"

— ISAIAH 64:1–2 KJV

…but refuse to rend our hearts before Him.

Even we His people are strangers to the Spirit of the fear of the Lord, and little trembling at His presence is present in many of our congregations.

Familiarity with God's presence and a shallow religion continues to caress us into a warm passivity that delights the devil.

Our Father does not require a simmering faith however, He is a consuming fire waiting for a people of zealous intent.

66 "For our God *is* a consuming fire."

— HEBREWS 12:29 KJV

The world may be cold to the demands of the gospel, but it is not only the coldness of the world that grieves God's heart - it is the lukewarm response of His children to the blazing promises He has placed before them.

Jesus warned:

> "I know thy works, that thou art neither cold nor hot: I would thou wert cold or hot.So then because thou art lukewarm, and neither cold nor hot, I will spue thee out of my mouth."

— REVELATION 3:15–16 KJV

Such hard words should shake us violently from our slumber.

Oh, that God would be gracious to us and send the Spirit of repentance to our hearts. Repentance not for this or that specific transgression, but a deep repentance at the very core of our being that changes our outlook with such dramatic clarity that Jesus becomes our all-in-all.

PART II
THE DIVINE PASSION - TO KNOW HIM

"I AM DEEPLY CONVINCED THAT THE NECESSITY OF PRAYER, IS NOT AS MUCH BASED ON OUR DESIRE FOR GOD AS ON GOD'S DESIRE FOR US. IT IS GOD'S PASSIONATE PURSUIT OF US THAT CALLS US TO PRAYER." — HENRI NOUWEN

"And this is life eternal, that they might know thee the only true God, and Jesus Christ, whom thou hast sent."

— JOHN 17:3 KJV

"TO KNOW HIM"

"THE ENGAGED MIND, ILLUMINATED BY TRUTH, AWAKENS AWARENESS; THE ENGAGED HEART, AFFECTED BY LOVE, AWAKENS PASSION...A FIERCE LONGING FOR GOD, AN UNYIELDING RESOLVE TO LIVE IN AND OUT OF OUR BELOVEDNESS." — BRENNAN MANNING

"Thus says the LORD: "Let not the wise man glory in his wisdom, Let not the mighty man glory in his might, Nor let the rich man glory in his riches; But let him who glories glory in this, That he understands and knows Me, That I am the LORD, exercising lovingkindness, judgment, and righteousness in the earth. for in these I delight." says the LORD."

— JEREMIAH 9:23,24, NKJV

Our passion should first be for God Himself, to know and to please Him. None were more passionate or purpose

47

driven than Paul the Apostle, yet the motivating force of his life was not the salvation of souls or turning the nations to righteousness. In the book of Philippians he reveals what undergirded his remarkable ministry:

> "Yet indeed I also count all things loss for the excellence of the knowledge of Christ Jesus my Lord, for whom I have suffered the loss of all things, and count them as rubbish, that I may gain Christ and be found in Him, not having my own righteousness, which is from the law, but that which is through faith in Christ, the righteousness which is from God by faith; that I may know Him and the power of His resurrection, and the fellowship of His sufferings, being conformed to His death, if, by any means, I may attain to the resurrection from the dead."
>
> — PHILIPPIANS 3:8-11, NKJV

To know Him.

As we make Jesus, and Jesus alone, the passionate pursuit of our hearts, we will naturally be propelled to zealously serve Him just as Paul did. Oftentimes our hearts grow weary in well-doing because we lose sight of the reason we are doing it.

Jesus is the reason. His love, His presence, His gospel.

When we take our eyes off the source and onto the work itself, we dry up. The real work of God, said Jesus, is simply to believe and walk with Him. Keeping our focus on the quality of our relationship, deriving our worth and affirmation from fellowship with Him, and only acting on His direction, ensures that we will not fall into the heavy yoke of self-reliance or mere religious observance.

The work of God is not burdensome.

66 "Jesus answered and said unto them, This is the work of God, that ye believe on him whom he hath sent."

— JOHN 6:29 KJV

How easy it us to forget the simplicity of the gospel we have been called to proclaim. How ever present the temptation to take out eyes off the 'Person' of God and get so caught up in the 'Purpose' of God we unplug from the Source of the love and power necessary to actually fulfill that purpose.

Oh God, turn our eyes to Jesus. Reveal Him to us. Show us His glory. Let us, with Paul, count all else as dung compared to knowing Him.

The Amplified Bible renders these same verses in Philippians so wonderfully:

> "Yes, furthermore, I count everything as loss compared to the possession of the priceless privilege (the overwhelming preciousness, the surpassing worth, and supreme advantage) of knowing Jesus Christ my Lord and of progressively becoming more deeply and intimately acquainted with Him [of perceiving and recognising and understanding Him more fully and clearly]. For His sake I have lost everything and consider it all to be mere rubbish (refuse, dregs), in order that I may win (gain) Christ (the Anointed One)...[for my determined purpose is] that I may know Him [that I may progressively become more deeply and intimately acquainted with Him,

perceiving and recognising and understanding the wonders of His Person more strongly and clearly], and that I may in that same way come to know the power outflowing from His resurrection [which it exerts over believers], and that I may so share His sufferings as to be continually transformed [in spirit into His likeness even] to His death, [in the hope] that if possible I may attain to the [spiritual and moral] resurrection [that lifts me] out from among the dead [even while in the body]."

The first commandment is so clear.

> "And you shall love the LORD your God with all your heart, with all your soul, with all your mind, and with all your strength.' This is the first commandment."

— MARK 12:30, NKJV

Fulfilment of the second command, to love your neighbor as yourself, flows from obedience to the first, loving God. If we have allowed Jesus' nature to flood our spirit and soul, we will inevitably grow in our fervent love for others.

The surest way to a genuine, lasting passion for God, and for His Kingdom, is to fall in love afresh with the King.

I love the words of a dear man of God who has influenced my prayer life in a wonderful way. He says this in one of his writings:

> "All other passions build upon or flow from your passion for Jesus. The most direct route to personal renewal and new effectiveness is a new all-consuming passion for Jesus. Lord, give us this passion, whatever the cost!"
>
> — *WESLEY L. DUEWEL*

Jesus is our all in all.

Jesus. Jesus. Jesus.

Notes & References Relevant to what you have just been reading:

Jeremiah 9:23-24; Philippians 3:8-11; Galatians 6:9; 2 Thessalonians 3:13; John 6:29; Philippians 3:8-11 Amplified Bible; Deuteronomy 6:5 and 10:12; Joshua 22:5; Matthew 22:37; mark 12:30; Luke 10:27; Romans 5:5

PICTURE YOUR PASSION

"MAY GOD GRANT US A DESIRE FOR GOD
THAT SUPERSEDES ALL OTHER DESIRES."
— A W TOZER

We read in the first part of this book about feeding our imagination with possibilities. Allowing the Holy Spirit to paint on the canvas of our mind positive pictures of the heavenly possibilities set before us. Consider for a moment these verses in Corinthians:

> "But as it is written: "Eye has not seen, nor ear heard, Nor have entered into the heart of man The things which God has prepared for those who love Him. But God has revealed them to us through His Spirit. For the Spirit searches all things, yes, the deep things of God. For what man knows the things of a man except

the spirit of the man which is in him? Even so no one knows the things of God except the Spirit of God. Now we have received, not the spirit of the world, but the Spirit who is from God, that we might know the things that have been freely given to us by God."

— 1 CORINTHIANS 2:9-12, NKJV

The natural mind hinders the flow of revelation. It downsizes God to the degree of our experience of Him, or to the things we have seen or heard others say. We fence Him in with the stance of our denomination or church movement, or by our formulas and doctrines. The truth is that God is much greater than any man could comprehend. Doctrine alone should never be the end game. Doctrine is important, essential even, but it should be experienced. We should be a people who not only know *about* God, we should actually *know* Him.

Sincerely pray that God would blast the barriers from your thinking, and that the Holy Spirit would stretch before you the panorama of God's good intentions for your lives, family, friends, city and nation. Revival, I believe, begins in the hearts and minds of those who apprehend what's possible. They see beyond the impossibilities that stand as obstacles, and look through a Holy Spirit inspired lens.

Don't meditate upon your own limitations. Do not dwell on the pitiful results you have witnessed after all the best efforts of your church. Give up those discouraging visions. Look instead to Jesus, the Author, Developer and Finisher of your faith.

Immerse yourself in the gospels. See who Jesus is. See how he lived and how he spoke. Consider His love, and meditate upon the results that flowed from His relationship with the Father. Take heart from His words in John 14:12 and John 20:21:

> "Most assuredly, I say to you, he who believes in Me, the works that I do he will do also; and greater works than these he will do, because I go to My Father."
>
> — JOHN 14:12, NKJV

> "So Jesus said to them again, Peace to you! As the Father has sent Me, I also send you."

— JOHN 20:21, NKJV

Shake off the shabby garment of past failures and frustrations and look again to Jesus. Men may fail us, movements may disappoint us, but Jesus never, never fails. He is the same yesterday, today and forever!

The very same things we witness in the Scriptures are God's normal. They may seem utterly extraordinary to us, but God is the Master of awesome. He wants to bring His children into a mighty ocean of revelation and experience, a deluge that floods our nations with citywide transformation.

Each and every saint is invited to play their vital part in the coming revival.

Let such thoughts humble our hearts and bring us to our knees with heartfelt petitions that God, our Heavenly Father, would move mercifully through our land. That His hand of kindness would heal the lands on which we stand.

"Come, dear Holy Spirit. Move on my heart that I might be lifted above the impossibilities. Sweep through my life with fresh and fervent desire for You and for your

purposes. Let me see so clearly what You want to do in my generation, like the joy that was set before Jesus - a joy that makes the sacrifice possible because the rewards are so tangible. Holy Spirit, dear friend and fire of Heaven, come flood my heart. Take the canvas of my heart and paint upon it all that you intend for your consecrated people."

Notes & References Relevant to what you have just been reading:

1 Corinthians 2:9-12; Hebrews 12:2; John 14:12; John 20:21; 1 Corinthians 13:8; Hebrews 13:8

PRAY YOUR PASSION (PART 1)

"A MAN MAY STUDY BECAUSE HIS BRAIN IS HUNGRY FOR KNOWLEDGE, EVEN BIBLE KNOWLEDGE. BUT HE PRAYS BECAUSE HIS SOUL IS HUNGRY FOR GOD." — LEONARD RAVENHILL

The prayer closet is the womb of revival - personal revival of dead passions, corporate revival in our churches, and sweeping national revivals that turn the tide of history.

The place of prayer is where we immerse our hearts in the purposes of God for our lives. It is where motives and intentions are sifted and purified, and where Jesus reveals His glory to our starving hearts.

It is important that we do not leave God-planted passions as unexpressed inward longings, because if we do they may end up as unhealthy frustrations. As we look at our apparent lack of intimacy with God, and seemingly impotent offerings of worship and service, we must not allow them to discourage, but rather provoke us to persistent prayer until we gain the prize and reward from heaven's storehouse. Yahweh is the God of the breakthrough.

Many promises have been given to all believers in this regard:

> "But without faith it is impossible to please Him, for he who comes to God must believe that He is, and that He is a rewarder of those who diligently seek Him."
>
> — HEBREWS 11:6, NKJV

> "And in that day you will ask Me nothing. Most assuredly, I say to you, whatever you ask the Father in My name He will give you."
>
> — JOHN 16:23, NKJV

> "And whatever you ask in My name, that I will do, that the Father may be glorified in the Son. If you ask anything in My name, I will do it."

— JOHN 14:13,14, NKJV

66 "And whatever things you ask in prayer, believing, you will receive."

— MATTHEW 21:22, NKJV

What awesome promises have been made available to us!

Are we prepared to translate our passion into persistent prayer, or will we merely let frustration build in our hearts?

It is a real danger when we perceive the shortcomings in the church that we would judge others as deficient and ignore the giant redwood poking from our own eye. There is a wise saying that states, "If you see something that needs to change, be the change." Revival does not begin with some new initiative or organized program of events, it occurs when the heart of an individual man or woman is moved to seek God with fervent intent.

Revival begins with us, and until we ourselves are genuinely aflame with the compassionate fire that burns in the heart of our Savior, blaming the state of the nation or the church is nothing less than hypocrisy.

I often say when the fingers are pointing and accusations fly, "the church should do this" or "the pastor should be more like that," that it is much like complaining about the traffic when we are stuck in tailback on the highway. Complain about the traffic all you like, you ARE the traffic! So it is when we complain about the church. You ARE the church.

The sooner we realize that the buck stops with us the simpler and better things will be. To your knees dear brother! To the closet my sister! The tide of prayer will rise when each living stone throws themselves wholeheartedly into the ocean of God's promises and begins to yearn earnestly for personal revival.

Let's turn our eyes to the all sufficient One, crying out to El-Shaddai to pour out His Spirit abundantly upon us. Don't point the finger and criticize others. Rather, intercede. Let your frustrations, disappointments and urgent questions be transformed by God's grace into a Godly tenacity that takes hold of Him as Jacob did crying, "I won't let go until You bless me!"

Open your heart and verbalize your deepest dreams, not as complaints because you are not seeing them happen, but as petitions before the throne of God until they do.

Jeremiah said;

> "Oh, that my head were waters, And my eyes a fountain of tears, That I might weep day and night For the slain of the daughter of my people!"

— JEREMIAH 9:1, NKJV

Pray that we too in our generation, would allow the weeping of God's heart to touch ours. That we too would cry the bitter tears of repentance in the light of God's goodness, to see our nation healed.

Is this not the cry of the bride for her Heavenly Bridegroom? Is this not why Jesus died? That men should know Him and be saved from sin? That the sick would be healed? That those slain and dying would be revived?

Let us pray and pray until.

Cast off religious restraint, passivity and political correctness and pour out your heart like water before the throne of grace.

"Have mercy, Lord. Send help in this, our time of need!"

What is our need?

"You, Lord! We need You!"

Notes & References Relevant to what you have just been reading:

2 Samuel 5:20 (Baal-Perazim means 'Lord of the Breakthrough'); Hebrews 11:6; John 16:23; John 14:13-14; Matthew 21:22; Matthew 7:2; Genesis 17:1 ('Almighty God' in Hebrew is El-Shaddai literally meaning "many breasted One", the All Sufficient One, the God of More Than Enough!); Genesis 32:26; Jeremiah 9:1; Romans 2:4; 1 Chronicles 7:14; Lamentations 2:19; Hebrews 4:16

PRAY YOUR PASSION (PART 2 - FASTING)

"I AM DEEPLY CONVINCED THAT THE NECESSITY OF PRAYER, IS NOT AS MUCH BASED ON OUR DESIRE FOR GOD AS ON GOD'S DESIRE FOR US. IT IS GOD'S PASSIONATE PURSUIT OF US THAT CALLS US TO PRAYER." — HENRI NOUWEN

Fasting, meaning primarily voluntary abstinence from food (and sometimes, but rarely, from water), is a very powerful way to press into God's presence and purpose for our lives. It helps us to take our focus from the natural to the spiritual aspect of our being.

Paul speaks in 1 Corinthians 9:27 about keeping the body in subjection to your spirit. The context of the verse is in relation to running the race of life successfully, and remaining focused in spite of our fight against the devil and the pressures exerted upon us by the flesh and the world.

David too speaks of fasting in Psalm 35:13. He used fasting as a means to 'humble' his soul. As we fast we declare our dependence on God, acknowledging our need for His presence and power. Such humility and poverty of spirit is pleasing in His sight.

> "If my people, which are called by my name, shall humble themselves, and pray, and seek my face, and turn from their wicked ways; then will I hear from heaven, and will forgive their sin, and will heal their land."
>
> — 2 CHRONICLES 7:14 KJV

If MY people, says God. We are God's people.

Humble themselves.

And pray.

Fasting causes a person's focus to turn toward the spirit and away from the flesh. It keeps the seeker alert to what is happening in the spiritual world. Oftentimes fasting aids breakthrough in prayer. Jesus Himself said that certain demons cannot be dislodged apart from the power released through prayer coupled with fasting.

In the pursuit of our 'prize', and as we run our race, many obstacles will present themselves; discouragements, setbacks, opportunities for offense. Focused fasting and fervent faith-filled prayer will keep us from succumbing to the schemes of the enemy. It will build our authority and ability to deal with and remove mountains in our path. A heart wholly given to God's presence is not good sticking ground for the fiery darts of the evil one.

How do we fast? First you need to understand that fasting is not some kind of glorified diet. It is a weapon that God has placed in the hands of believers to accomplish things in the spiritual realm that nothing else can.

Consider Isaiah 58:6-13 that lists some of the benefits of fasting. These include removing heavy burdens, breaking yokes of slavery, and a powerfully acute ability to converse with God.

I started to highlight the rich promises contained in these verses but had to stop because every word was worthy of emphasis. I encourage you to read them carefully. Meditate upon them until faith arises in your heart to appropriate what the Father says about His kind of fast:

"Is this not the fast that I have chosen:

To loose the bonds of wickedness,

To undo the heavy burdens,

To let the oppressed go free,

And that you break every yoke?

Is it not to share your bread with the hungry,

And that you bring to your house the poor who are cast out;

When you see the naked, that you cover him,

And not hide yourself from your own flesh?

Then your light shall break forth like the morning,

Your healing shall spring forth speedily,

And your righteousness shall go before you;

The glory of the LORD shall be your rear guard.

Then you shall call, and the LORD will answer;

You shall cry, and He will say, "Here I *am.*'

'If you take away the yoke from your midst,

The pointing of the finger, and speaking wickedness,

If you extend your soul to the hungry

And satisfy the afflicted soul,

Then your light shall dawn in the darkness,

And your darkness shall *be* as the noonday.

The LORD will guide you continually,

And satisfy your soul in drought,

And strengthen your bones;

You shall be like a watered garden,

And like a spring of water, whose waters do not fail.

Those from among you shall build the old waste places;

You shall raise up the foundations of many generations;

And you shall be called the Repairer of the Breach,

The Restorer of Streets to Dwell In.

"If you turn away your foot from the Sabbath,

From doing your pleasure on My holy day,

And call the Sabbath a delight,

The holy *day* of the LORD honorable,

And shall honor Him, not doing your own ways,

Nor finding your own pleasure,

Nor speaking *your own* words,"

(Isaiah 58:6–13 NKJV)

Over the years I have found that a strong sense of purpose, and a recognition of what God promises, is essential to successful fasting. If your spiritual hunger to see victory in your chosen goal outweighs your natural desire for food, you will succeed and see clear results. Purposeless fasting often ends in disappointment. We blow it because we don't have our eyes fixed on a greater goal when the hunger pangs strike. Fix your eyes on the goal, perhaps the salvation of a loved one, a renewed relationship with God, and do not waver, knowing that God will move on your behalf.

Set yourself realistic goals with God's direction. It is better to successfully fast three days with your heart engaged in faith, than striving to do fifteen days and stumble through full of doubt, and then blow it on day five feeling like a big failure.

There are all sorts of fast that you can engage in. Daniel, the Old Testament prophet, set himself to fast for twenty-one days eating only very plain food. His requests were gloriously and supernaturally granted.

Esther and the Jewish people fasted three days and three nights without food or water (fasting without water is inadvisable unless specifically directed by God). Their goal was miraculously achieved, their petitions answered and an entire nation saved. Yours can be too!

I know people who fast 20-30 days on a regular basis, others who eat one day, fast the next (effectively six months per year). Others eat only one meal per day. Some fast a certain number of meals per week. Marilyn Hickey, a Bible teacher from the US, fasts seven meals per week. This kind of fast can be done a few meals some days and less on others, or by simply missing any one meal each day. It is very flexible.

You may want to fast just part of a day, say until 1pm or 4pm. I personally like to fast 4-5 days, eating no food at all, but drinking as I please.

Find what works for you. The key is not how many days or how you fast, but that your heart is positioned in a faithful and expectant stance toward your Heavenly Father when you do so.

Jesus did not say, "by your discipline be it not you." He said, "by your faith be it unto you..." (Mark 9:29)

Notes & References Relevant to what you have just been reading:

1 Chronicles 9:27; Psalm 35:13; James 4:10; Matthew 5:3; Matthew 17:21; 2 Corinthians 2:11; Luke 10:19; mark 11:22-33; Romans 16:20; Ephesians 6:16; Isaiah 58:6-13; Matthew 6:16-18; Daniel 10:3; Esther 4:16

PERSIST IN YOUR PASSION

"IT WOULD SEEM THAT OUR LORD FINDS
OUR DESIRES NOT TOO STRONG, BUT TOO
WEAK. WE ARE HALF-HEARTED
CREATURES, FOOLING ABOUT WITH DRINK
AND SEX AND AMBITION WHEN INFINITE
JOY IS OFFERED US, LIKE AN IGNORANT
CHILD WHO WANTS TO GO ON MAKING
MUD PIES IN A SLUM BECAUSE HE CANNOT
IMAGINE WHAT IS MEANT BY THE OFFER
OF A HOLIDAY AT THE SEA. WE ARE FAR
TOO EASILY PLEASED." — C. S. LEWIS

"Behold, I send My messenger And he will prepare the way before Me. And the Lord, whom you seek Will suddenly come to His temple, Even the Messenger of the covenant In whom you delight. Behold, He is coming, Says the LORD of hosts."

— MALACHI 3:1, NKJV

Consistency and patience are essential ingredients to our development in the things of God. He is more like a farmer, and certainly not a magician pulling rabbits from hats. Christian life is agricultural in nature, not a fast-cook microwave meal. Seed takes time to root, sprout, grow and bear fruit. We must be willing to stick with this thing until. We need to work closely with the Holy Spirit and honor His timings for our lives. Who are we, the pot, to question the potter?

Jesus Himself told a parable warning against this tendency to go just part way and then give up. See Luke chapter 18. Luke interprets the purpose of the parable Jesus told in this way: "And he spake a parable unto them *to this end*, that men ought always to pray, and not to faint;"

Peter talked of those who mock the Word and promise of God, and how essential it is for us to persevere despite circumstances that appear contrary to our believing. Rarely is a revival preceded by a garden of roses. Many times the backdrop of revival is pitch darkness. A desperation in the face of insurmountable odds is often the very goad that pushes men to depths of prayer that finally break through.

> "Knowing this first, that there shall come in the last days scoffers, walking after their own lusts,And saying, Where is the promise of his coming?"
>
> — 2 PETER 3:3–4 KJV

The reason for God's apparent delay is not unwillingness to act, it is an overriding compassion that none would perish:

> "The Lord is not slack concerning his promise, as some men count slackness; but is longsuffering to us-ward, not willing that any should perish, but that all should come to repentance."
>
> — 2 PETER 3:9 KJV

He is holding the coming of His Son so we, like the generation of Noah, have room to repent. They of course did not. Dear God, may it not be so in our day!

Help us, Lord, not to be part of that critical company of men who shun your promises. Let us not be like the steward in Matthew 24:44-51 who threw off his stewardship because His Master's return was delayed.

Friend, now is not the time to resign. Now is not the time to give in to discouragement. If ever there was an hour that demanded renewed zeal it is now!

It is through faith AND patience that we inherit the promises.

Again and again throughout scripture we see how God came suddenly to a believer or a group of believers. God's reward comes to the faithful. They were doing what they had always done, but 'suddenly' everything changed. God turned up!

We witness God's arrival in Acts the second chapter.

> "When the Day of Pentecost had fully come, they were all with one accord in one place. And **suddenly there came a sound from heaven, as of a rushing mighty wind, and it filled the whole house where they were sitting.** Then there appeared to them divided tongues,

as of fire, and one sat upon each of them. And they were all filled with the Holy Spirit and began to speak with other tongues, as the Spirit gave them utterance."

— ACTS 2:1-4

The disciples were 'tarrying' as Jesus had commanded. One hundred and twenty remained to see the glorious appearing of God's Holy Ghost among them. I wonder how many gave up and left before that moment? It was several days after Jesus had been taken from them. Maybe on day five, Joseph-bar-Bloggs decided that he'd had enough and slipped back out to work. Possibly on day seven, a group decided that nothing was happening so they'd go for a dip in the local spa. Who knows? What we do know is, without warning, and all of a sudden, this group of 120 men and women came face-to-face with the consuming Fire of God. As a result the entire world was changed.

We must ensure we are present for God's appointments in our lives. When we sense the drawing of the Holy Spirit to intimacy, we must respond. Maybe your own suddenly is awaiting you in an ordained but as-yet undisclosed place of revelation.

When Jesus was born the shepherds had their 'suddenly'. Until that time it was a regular night's work watching the sheep. But...

> "...**suddenly there was with the angel a multitude of the heavenly host praising God** and saying: "Glory to God in the highest, And on earth peace, goodwill toward men!""

— LUKE 2:13,14, NKJV

Saul, the persecutor of the church, later known as Paul the Apostle had his 'suddenly' on the road to Damascus;

> "Now it happened, as I journeyed and came near Damascus at about noon, **suddenly a great light from heaven shone** around me."

— ACTS 22:6, NKJV

Indeed, all men will one day experience the ultimate 'suddenly' of them all;

> "Therefore you also be ready, for **the Son of Man is coming at an hour you do not expect**."

— LUKE 12:40, NKJV

What about you? Are you expecting a meeting with the Living God? Men and women who have encountered the realities of Heaven accomplish great things for the Kingdom. What we can accomplish in our own strength and talent is so limited. Real fruit comes only through encountering Jesus.

I want to meet with Him. I know my 'suddenly' is coming. As I remain faithful, and pace my floor crying for more. One day. Suddenly. He will come. I want Jesus. I want God. I'm hungry. Stay with it. Follow the hunger pangs of your heart until you meet with His presence. Don't give up before the time. Ask for the spiritual rain. Do not settle for a few choice drops when He wants to send a deluge.

Asuza Street in Los Angeles saw an awesome move of God in the early 1900's. God came suddenly.

Immediately prior to this, Evan Roberts prayer, "Bend us, Lord" sparked a sudden and sweeping revival that turned Wales upside down for the gospel. Indeed, between 1904-1905 all of Wales was moved Godward. Bars were closed, movie houses shut down, ungodly curses in miner's mouths were transformed to heavenly praise. Within a few short years converts numbered 100,000.

The real revival began in Evan Robert's heart when, in the Spring of 1904, he had what he calls his 'day of visitation'. In the privacy of his own room in Loughor, Wales, he says, *"The Holy Spirit manifested Himself in an overwhelming manner which filled my soul with divine awe."* It was shortly after this, in September, that, along with nineteen other young people at Blaenanerch, Wales, Evan prayed the famous prayer, "Bend us, Oh Lord!" That moment was to become the turning point not only for Evan, but for entire nations.

More recently we have witnessed significant outpourings in parts of the USA, Columbia, Argentina, Uganda and Fiji, to name just a few. In every case the outpouring came after many months of intensive prayer.

These are just a few instances of God's *'suddenlies'* which have turned the tides of history. I encourage you to get hold of the 'Transformations' documentaries accounting of some of these marvelous modern revivals (produced by the Sentinel Group http://www.sentinelgroup.org).

As the Scriptures say:

> "After they prayed, the place where they were meeting was shaken."

— ACTS 4:31 NIV

We cannot do the shaking, but we can do the praying! The timings are in the Lord's hand, but every outpouring of God's power has always been precipitated by prayer.

When men and women commit to persevere in faithfulness and prayer great and mighty things occur. God answers with power.

The disciples were "with one accord in prayer and supplication" before the Pentecost outpouring. The

Wales and Asuza revivals too, were preceded by passionate, lengthy heartfelt prayer; sometimes weeks, sometimes months, often years. But the suddenly came. I believe that there is a 'suddenly' for our nation today. Our heart hunger and fervent prayer calls it forth.

In no way am I saying stop what you are currently doing. Stay faithful, do what you know to be right, but don't settle for less than God Himself moving in your midst. Persevere in your passion and pursuit.

God has promised open reward to those who 'earnestly and diligently' seek Him.

Notes & References Relevant to what you have just been reading:

Malachi 3:1; Hebrews 6:12; Hebrews 10:35,39; Matthew 13:18-23; Luke 8:10-15; Jeremiah 18:1-6; Romans 9:20; Luke 18:1-8; Luke 12:35-48; 2 Peter 3:3-13; Hebrews 6:12; Acts 2:1-4; Luke 24:49; Acts 1:15; Luke 2:13-14; Acts 22:6; Acts 9:1-19; Luke 12:35-40; Matthew 24:36-25:13; Zechariah 10:1; Acts 1:14; Hebrews 11:6

EYES ON ETERNITY

"YOU ARE PROBABLY AT YOUR SANEST
WHEN YOU COME TO THE PLACE WHERE
YOU ABANDON ALL ELSE BUT YOUR DESIRE
FOR GOD." — R. T. KENDALL

My devotional reading brought me to the chapters in Matthew where Jesus speaks about the end times. Chapters 24 and 25 of Matthew deep dive the subject with directions and parables to prepare our Hearts for His coming. In Mark 13, Jesus spoke around the subject again. He urged his disciples to 'watch and pray'.

"Take ye heed, watch and pray: for ye know not when the time is."

— MARK 13:33 KJV

Such things are choice reminders to keep our eyes on eternal things rather than just the temporal. This life, for all of its urgent insistent pleas, is really nothing more than a breath in eternity. "Poof!" And it's over - we step into our real life.

Life here is preparation for there. Life now is training for life then. What we do in these short moments will determine our place and position in eternity.

These thoughts arose as I pondered the mystery of seemingly unanswered prayer in relation to the purpose of God. I was reminded as I read Matthew and other passages relating to the final spasms of earth's present age, that Papa is preparing us for far greater things than we can ever comprehend. He is shaping our character for eternity, training us for reigning.

Sometimes our limited perspective symbolically sees only the end of our own nose. We see our pressing needs, feel our pain and wrestle with perplexities. But God has a greater purpose at work. He is forming our character for eternity.

Humans are made by God to rule. We naturally build kingdoms; businesses, churches, reputations, wealth and fame. God Himself placed this Kingdom-building gene within the original man, Adam. He commanded Him to take dominion.

The problem is, after the fall, mankind still builds kingdoms, but often neglect to build the character necessary to rightly rule those kingdoms. Character over kingdom should be our mode of operation. We must allow Father to shape our character, knowing that the real rulership is not in this sandbox we exist in called time. No, we are being built for eternal responsibilities.

From this perspective we view the challenges differently. We embrace success and failure with equal submission to God's masterful hand. I'm not saying this is easy, or that I do it well, but I certainly want to allow the Holy Spirit the privilege to lift my eyes above the moment I'm presently experiencing. I want to be a man like Paul who was able to honestly say that he had found the grace to be content whatever his situation.

> "Not that I speak in respect of want: for I have learned, in whatsoever state I am, *therewith* to be content."

> — PHILIPPIANS 4:11 KJV

Paul was neither moved by privilege or by privation. His measure was not the same as the one world uses. His estimation of success was not weighed by the world's gauge. Nor should these false worldly weights be the ones that we judge our worth by.

In the culture we are soaked in, the measures of success, even spiritual success, are counted in dollars and numbers, in titles and badges of honor.

In the early church the honor roll was VERY (emphasis is deliberate!) different.

> "And they departed from the presence of the council, rejoicing that they were counted worthy to suffer shame for his name."
>
> — ACTS 5:41 KJV

> "And I saw thrones, and they sat upon them, and judgment was given unto them: and *I saw* the souls of them that were beheaded for the witness of Jesus, and for the word of God, and which had not worshipped the beast, neither his image..."

— REVELATION 20:4 KJV

These are just a tiny handful of hundreds of verses that challenge the skewed cultural emphasis we place on success, accumulation, and vain acclamation.

The day of Jesus' judgement will turn the world on its head, with the first being last and the last first. Some of the most invisible and seemingly downtrodden saints today will sit on thrones, whilst those who wear the crowns in this life are left to clean their shoes.

If you want to cultivate a passion that surpasses the world's bids for your affection, the only way to do so is have a perspective rooted in the age to come. An eternal future for which you are now being shaped. Circumstances, whether good or bad, are often the brawny hands that pummel the clay into its final form; a vessel beautifully shaped for the Master's use.

There are some verses that you rarely find in the promise boxes of positivity and prosperity. They are not the ones we claim and confess. But they sit unashamed alongside other proclamations of God's love and victory in our lives. As A W Tozer said, only the whole of Scripture can make a whole Christian.

> "Though he were a Son, yet learned he obedience by the things which he suffered;"
>
> — HEBREWS 5:8 KJV

> "Ye have not yet resisted unto blood, striving against sin.And ye have forgotten the exhortation which speaketh unto you as unto children, My son, despise not thou the chastening of the Lord, nor faint when thou art rebuked of him:For whom the Lord loveth he chasteneth, and scourgeth every son whom he receiveth."
>
> — HEBREWS 12:3–6 KJV

Maybe it is time to revisit our Bibles and read and pray through all of the verses we DID NOT underline.

I love, and I am challenged by, Peter's exhortation to any serious disciple of Jesus Christ. Notice in the following verses that the emphasis is on development of character, not the building of an ecclesiastical empire.

"And because of his glory and excellence, he has given us great and precious promises. These are the promises that enable you to share his divine nature and escape the world's corruption caused by human desires.

In view of all this, make every effort to respond to God's promises. Supplement your faith with a generous provision of moral excellence, and moral excellence with knowledge, and knowledge with self-control, and self-control with patient endurance, and patient endurance with godliness, and godliness with brotherly affection, and brotherly affection with love for everyone.

The more you grow like this, the more productive and useful you will be in your knowledge of our Lord Jesus Christ.But those who fail to develop in this way are shortsighted or blind, forgetting that they have been cleansed from their old sins."

— 2 PETER 1:4–9 NLT

Religious empires will fall, and even the good will be shaken and taken when the Lord returns. The stewardships we have undertaken will be returned to the Master, and it will be our character that we carry into the new Heaven and earth ready for the real work to begin.

Let's keep our eyes on eternity.

How powerfully motivating and counter-cultural are these prayerful verses from Colossians in the New Living Translation:

> "Since you have been raised to new life with Christ, **set your sights on the realities of heaven, where Christ sits in the place of honor at God's right hand. Think about the things of heaven, not the things of earth.** For you died to this life, and your real life is hidden with Christ in God. And when Christ, who is your life, is revealed to the whole world, you will share in all his glory."

— COLOSSIANS 3:1–4 NLT

Take these words and dig them deep into your heart, so that they become the frame through which you judge your world. In the light of eternity the things that appear important and significant change dramatically. When this shift takes place within us, we also change dramatically.

The beautiful words of John reveal how having our eyes on the realities of Heaven and its inhabitants changes us:

> "Behold, what manner of love the Father hath bestowed upon us, that we should be called the sons of God: therefore the world knoweth us not, because it knew him not. Beloved, now are we the sons of God, and it doth not yet appear what we shall be: but we know that, when he shall appear, we shall be like him; for we shall see him as he is. And every man that hath this hope in him purifieth himself, even as he is pure."
>
> — 1 JOHN 3:1–3 KJV

Sure, we may be misunderstood. We may even be labeled fanatical by well meaning brothers and sisters. But dear brethren, as the things of earth grow dim in your sight and eternity shines ever brighter, Jesus will become your all in all.

Jesus! Jesus! Jesus!

Again.

Jesus!

PART III
THE MINISTRY OF JESUS

"The Gospel is not an old, old story, freshly told. It is a fire in the Spirit, fed by the flame of Immortal Love; and woe unto us, if, through our negligence to stir up the Gift of God which is within us, that fire burns low."

— **LEONARD RAVENHILL, WHY REVIVAL TARRIES**

THE MINISTRY OF JESUS

ALL OTHER PASSIONS BUILD UPON OR
FLOW FROM YOUR PASSION FOR JESUS. A
PASSION FOR SOULS GROWS OUT OF A
PASSION FOR CHRIST. A PASSION FOR
MISSIONS BUILDS UPON A PASSION FOR
CHRIST. THE MOST CRUCIAL DANGER TO A
CHRISTIAN, WHATEVER HIS ROLE, IS TO
LACK A PASSION OF CHRIST. THE MOST
DIRECT ROUTE TO PERSONAL RENEWAL
AND NEW EFFECTIVENESS IS A NEW ALL-
CONSUMING PASSION FOR JESUS. LORD,
GIVE US THIS PASSION, WHATEVER THE
COST! — WESLEY L DUEWEL

Biblically, if you are a believer, you are a minister. I hope you realize that.

Although people talk about ministries, in truth there is only one ministry, and many stewards of that one ministry. It is the ministry of Jesus Christ. We are privileged, as children of God, to share in that ministry.

It was His ministry when He walked the earth, and it is still His today as He walks the earth in and through us.

I once had an unusual vision. It was humorous but very profound. I saw myself entering Heaven. Standing before me was an angel dressed as a border guard - a customs official. He was beside one of those machines that you see in airports where you are required to place your bags and the contents of your pockets before stepping through the metal detectors.

I stood there at heaven's border control, having placed the obvious items on the conveyor, and was about to step through when the angel reached out his hand to stop me. He pointed to several badges I was wearing.

"Pastor", "Home Group Leader", "Intercessor", "Bible teacher", "Counsellor"…

Many of the roles I had played in my years of service. The badges of honor that we so often pridefully wear.

"You need to give those up, " he said. "They don't belong to you."

Each one had to be returned to its true owner; Jesus.

It was His ministry. Always was. And I was merely a steward for a short season.

Upon our return home, all that belongs to Him must be given back to Him. I don't step into Heaven as a pastor. None of the temporary roles I play here cross that line. I walk into His presence as naked as the day I was born, with nothing but Jesus to commend me.

This does not mean I won't be rewarded. It does not mean that your service and sacrifice is worthless. It simply means that these are not the things that define you.

The idea that there is a set-apart elite force, who alone are called to carry out the heavenly commission is alien to the scriptures. Those called to the ministry offices as described in Ephesians are called to equip everyone else, every single believer, to do the job. It is the work of the prophet, apostle, pastor, teacher and evangelist to equip you and I for the 'work of the ministry'.

So what is 'the ministry'?

The calling of God is far greater and more impossible than singing a few songs or teaching some encouraging messages. In fact, the believer's ministry is so outrageous that every one of us is thrown into the same boat, whatever level of talent, gifting or training we may or may not have.

The name of the boat? "Helpless"

The prayer of its passengers, "Help!"

The response of its captain, "POWER!"

Let's look together at scripture:

> "Now all things are of God, who has reconciled us to Himself through Jesus Christ, and has given us the ministry of reconciliation, that is, that God was in Christ reconciling the world to Himself, not imputing their trespasses to them, and has committed to us the word of reconciliation. Now then, we are ambassadors for Christ, as though God were pleading through us: we implore you on Christ's behalf, be reconciled to God."
>
> — 2 CORINTHIANS 5:18-20, NKJV

We are called as ambassadors for Christ.

Our ministry? To reconcile others to Him.

We all should be telling others about the Lord and His plan of redemption. Furthermore, we should be able to prove by supernatural demonstration the truth that we proclaim.

> "And He said to them, "Go into all the world and preach the gospel to every creature. "He who believes and is baptized will be saved; but he who does not believe will be condemned. "And these signs will follow those who believe: In My name they will cast out demons; they will speak with new tongues; "they will take up serpents; and if they drink anything deadly, it will by no means hurt them; they will lay hands on the sick, and they will recover.""

— MARK 16:15-18, NKJV

Outlined here is the ministry of the believer. It is not the ministry of the apostle alone, or the special anointing of the mass evangelist. No, this is the ministry calling of the regular believer in Jesus!

Here again we are thrown on the mercy of the Lord Himself. How can we boast in ourselves or our talents when, of our own strength, we cannot even fulfil the very first requirements of God's ministry for us?

We may be a 'teacher' but as we teach we ought to be seeing demons flee, sickness healed and men reached radically for God. We may be a 'song-leader' but if we're not breaking chains of iniquity what are we accomplishing more than the local rock band in the pub down the road?

Ministry positions and titles in and of themselves, all the accolades of church life as we know them today, are worthless. Our commendation must come from God and not from men.

The following verse is one that challenges me deeply:

> "[Besides this evidence] it was also established *and* plainly endorsed by God, Who showed His approval of it by signs and wonders and various miraculous manifestations of [His] power and by imparting the gifts of the Holy Spirit [to the believers] according to His own will."

— HEBREWS 2:4 AMP

God's commendation is supernatural in nature.

As we seek to be a true witness (one who presents the truth with evidence) we will have our focus on the True and not some cleverly concocted religious counterfeit. Let us cast away all our boastings and humble ourselves before the Father until we experience in our individual and corporate lives the overflow of the real and only authentic ministry on the planet - His ministry!

In all of this, I'm looking myself squarely in the mirror yearning for the gap between what the Bible teaches and my experience of it to be brought ever closer together.

Jesus! Jesus! Jesus! Have Your way in us!

We want to RE-PRESENT You to the world. We want to show them what YOU can do. We want to be YOUR mouthpiece.

Have your glorious way through your Church, Lord!

Notes & References Relevant to what you have just been reading:

2 Corinthians 6:16; 2 Corinthians 5:18-20; Mark 16:15-18; 1 Thessalonians 1:5; 1 Corinthians 2:4-5; 2 Corinthians 2:4-5; 2 Corinthians 10:12-18; Acts 1:8; John 15:1-5

EMPTY VESSELS

"LORD STRENGTHEN ME WHERE I AM TOO
WEAK AND WEAKEN ME WHERE I AM TOO
STRONG!" — LEONARD RAVENHILL

God can only pour into our emptiness. If we are full of ourselves; our plans and our opinions, we leave no room for the Lord to fill. In 2 Kings 4:1-7 the supply of oil dried up when all the vessels were full. God wants us full too, but not with ourselves. He wants to fill us with His Spirit so our lives can be poured out in love and service to others.

Continually we need to come before the Lord to be filled again. Without Him we can do nothing.

In the book of Revelation Jesus speaks by the Spirit to the seven churches. Many commentators believe that the seven churches mentioned in these chapters represent seven church ages. The age in which we live is compared to the 'Laodicean' church.

> "...you say, 'I am rich, have become wealthy, and have need of nothing' - and do not know that you are wretched, miserable, poor, blind, and naked- I counsel you to buy from Me gold refined in the fire, that you may be rich; and white garments, that you may be clothed, that the shame of your nakedness may not be revealed; and anoint your eyes with eye salve, that you may see."
>
> — REVELATION 3:17-18, NKJV

Acknowledging our weakness puts us in a position to receive His strength. Admitting our poverty of spirit places us a possessors of Heaven's rich supply. We can only say we are strong because of Jesus. We can only declare our wealth because of Him, because true wealth is spiritual not natural.

When I was a child, there was a children's program on TV here in the UK called "Let's Pretend". In it, kids would dress up and role play different imaginative games, pretending to be kings and queens or whatever. I fear that the modern church, particularly in affluent Western cultures, are playing the same game. We come dressed with all the church-speak, knowing just what to say and how to act. We hold 'revival' services and celebrate the great 'move of the Spirit' that we are supposedly experiencing. But where is the revival? Is the Spirit really moving as powerfully as we would like everyone to believe? Or are we, like the Laodicean's, vainly bragging like the emperor in His new clothes. The church stands by applauding, while the world, like the little boy in the crowd, stands and points out that the emperor has 'no clothes on'!

Please don't misunderstand. We are experiencing God working in our midst. People's lives are being deeply impacted for the Lord. This is true, and we must always be thankful for everything that reflects the awesome grace of God transform sinners into saints.

But we are talking here about a matter of degrees. Are the people falling under conviction of sin in the streets? Are our neighbors smitten with the fear of the Lord when they hear us worshipping the Lord next door? Do our church services overflow with hungry seekers? Do our prayers really shake the world?

So long as we soothe ourselves with excuses, or choose comfortable familiarity over honestly challenging the status quo, we strip ourselves of any virility in the prayer closet. Our prayers will remain lukewarm and self-satisfied.

Leonard Ravenhill was a revivalist preacher known for his forthright message. He said:

> "No man is greater than his prayer life. The pastor who is not praying is playing; the people who are not praying are straying. We have many organizers, but few agonizers; many players and payers, few pray-ers; many singers, few clingers; lots of pastors, few wrestlers; many fears, few tears; much fashion, little passion; many interferers, few intercessors; many writers, but few fighters. Failing here, we fail everywhere."

Let's get honest with ourselves and with God. In true humility of heart weep with the elders between the porch and the altar until we all see what our hearts so desperately crave.

Notes & References Relevant to what you have just been reading:

2 Kings 4:1-7; 2 Timothy 4:6; Revelation 3:14-22; Matthew 5:3; Joel 3:10; Joel 2:17-18

SOULS SOULS SOULS - NO LONGER PASSIVE, BUT PASSIONATE!

> "IF YOU HAD THE CURE TO CANCER WOULDN'T YOU SHARE IT? ... YOU HAVE THE CURE TO DEATH ... GET OUT THERE AND SHARE IT." — KIRK CAMERON

The surface waters of life include all the day-to-day chores and responsibilities, but underneath there must be a mighty subterranean river flowing through the motivations of our life. The deep places must call out for the deep things of God.

Jesus once spoke and said that He has called me to provoke people to pursuit and purity. I was conflicted about how intense I sometimes come across, thinking that I should be some other way. But God wires us all uniquely, and when I brought my concerns to Him, He affirmed the restless pursuit that often drives my heart to seek Him further. I guess confrontational messages are just part of my call, but be certain that I am confronting myself more than any other.

I choose to confront myself with hard questions that search my heart and sift my motives. The Bible says that our hearts can be very devious if left to their own devices, and although we become new creations in Christ Jesus this tendency toward self-justification often spills over into the new life.

The Word of God encourages us to "judge ourselves" in the light of scripture, and allow the sharp two-edged sword of Truth to sift the motives of our heart.

> "For the Word that God speaks is alive and full of power [making it active, operative, energising, and effective]; it is sharper than any two-edged sword, penetrating to the dividing line of the breath of life (soul) and [the immortal] spirit, and of joints and marrow [of the deepest parts of our nature], exposing and sifting and analyzing and judging the very thoughts and purposes of the heart."

> — HEBREWS 4:12, AMPLIFIED

Blood-bought brothers and sisters indeed ought to be provocative in the right sense of the word:

> "And let us consider one another to provoke unto love and to good works:"

— HEBREWS 10:24 KJV

Notice that when we honestly consider one another we will incite each other to pursue God and serve Him wholeheartedly. It is so easy to get so wrapped up in the temporal affairs of this life that eternal considerations are sidelined. It takes Christian fellowship to keep the flames of passion burning brightly. A lone twig from the fire left apart will soon fizzle out. Place burning logs together and their flames feed one another until the whole is ablaze. We need one another and we must not be afraid to speak honestly and challenge ourselves to take the things of God seriously. Jesus is coming soon, and our hearts of love for the King and our service to the Kingdom must be ready for that day.

We are called to share the warm heat of our heart for God with each other and feed one another's flames toward fervency.

Developing a passion for God may be cultivated alone in the prayer closet, but it is multiplied and brought to fullness only in fellowship with like-minded and like-hearted believers.

I have made it a point to seek out a handful of men in whom I recognize a genuine hunger for the things of God, and then prioritize meeting with them regularly. We make ourselves accountable to one another, pray for one another, and do all we can to continually encourage each another to more passionate pursuit and service in the Kingdom of our Father.

In exposing and sifting the motives of the heart , a great question to ask yourself is one of the simplest to ask, but the hardest to answer; "Why?"

Why do you do the things that you do? What significance will your actions and activities have from an eternal perspective?

It strikes me that if we believed with all of our heart even half of what we claim, we would live radically different lifestyles. If our neighbors, friends, family and work colleagues are going to Hell with no hope apart from Christ, wouldn't we do all we can to reach them? Would our energies not be spent in heartfelt intercession, and our lives be moved with compassion to reach the lost at any cost?

Our commission is to "Go into all the world and preach the gospel" but often we are hard-pushed to even go to our next door neighbor. For some even going to church on Sunday is an overwhelming effort!

If we really believed that it is the believer's right and authority to lay hands on the sick and see them healed, no sick or crippled person would cross our path without us making the good news of healing available to them. Indeed, they would be seeking out the churches knowing that is the place where they could find healing and deliverance from their afflictions.

I also realize that this kind of shift is not something we can muster up in our strength of will. It must come from Heaven. It is the gift of God, available to anyone who seeks Him with all of their heart.

> "Then shall ye call upon me, and ye shall go and pray unto me, and I will hearken unto you. And ye shall seek me, and find *me*, when ye shall search for me with all your heart. And I will be found of you,

saith the LORD: and I will turn away
your captivity..."

— JEREMIAH 29:12–14 KJV

Sometimes we live with such a passive insistence in
the sovereignty of God, thinking that He will do as
He pleases with or without our intervention. But the
Scriptures are replete with a theology that is so
contrary to this fatalistic and downright lazy point
of view.

God is moved when His people are moved!

His ear is attentive to our cry!

"Call unto me, and I will answer thee, and
shew thee great and mighty things, which
thou knowest not."

— JEREMIAH 33:3 KJV

Ask Father today to give you the desires of His heart.
To plant them so deeply within you that you cannot
remain the same. Oh, that we would *really* be moved
by the things that move Him. That *our* inner world

would be turned upside down so we could be used to turn the world outside.

Let's be active in our faith. Let our lives display like billboards what we believe. Let our passion for the Lord thrust us into the harvest of souls starving in the wilderness of this sinful world, and bring them by the sheave into the Kingdom of our wonderful God.

Seek Him with all of your heart. Step out of your comfort zone. Pray more. Organize your days around what you know to be significant, not around the trifles of life. Get out of your comforts and share the Good News. Call your unsaved friends and invite them for a meal, all the while looking for opportunities and open doors to share your testimony of God's goodness. When God becomes more real to us, it will be perfectly natural for us to share our stories of His grace and intervention.

Let's live this thing, giving ourselves uncompromisingly to the call of Heaven. Teamed together with the Holy Spirit there is nothing that is impossible for us. By our faith we can see Jesus hit the streets and homes of our nation.

This is our generation. This is our time. We live our lives once and then the judgement. Let's make them count!

Notes & References Relevant to what you have just been reading:

Psalm 42:7; Jeremiah 17:9; 1 Corinthians 11:31; James 1:23-25; Hebrews 4:12; Matthew 28:18-20; Mark 16:15; Mark 16:18; 1 John 4:4; 2 Chronicles 16:9; John 7:17; Matthew 9:38; Luke 10:2; Jeremiah 29:13; 2 Timothy 4:5; Matthew 17:20; Luke 1:27; Mark 9:23; Hebrews 9:27

DISCOVER THE SECRETS OF THE HEAVENLY TABERNACLE...

Free Tabernacle Prayer Guide & Video Workshop

www.davidleemartin.net/tabernacle-prayer-guide

Your free illustrated guide to Tabernacle Prayer, leading you step-by-step through this powerful pathway to the Father's presence.

Also includes Free Access to an in-depth online prayer workshop.

Recorded at a full day of Tabernacle Prayer teaching and activation, these powerful video sessions lead the listener through the gates of the Heavenly Tabernacle on a revelation filled journey into the Holy of Holies.

You will learn to pray Tabernacle Prayer with 4 hours of in depth revelatory teaching, activation and life-changing testimony.

Join David For A Life-Changing Revelation of Prayer and Encounter With God
www.davidleemartin.net/tabernacle-prayer-guide

Printed in Great Britain
by Amazon

16447619R00070